groove

DILEMMAS

GROOVE: DILEMMAS

Groove is published by Youth Ministry Partners and Abingdon Press, The United Methodist Publishing House, 2222 Rosa L. Parks Blvd., P.O. Box 280988, Nashville, TN 37228-0988. Copyright © 2015 Youth Ministry Partners and Abingdon Press.

Scripture quotations unless noted otherwise are from the Common English Bible. Copyright © 2011 by the Common English Bible. All rights reserved. Used by permission. (*CommonEnglishBible.com*)

Scripture quotations marked (NIV) are taken from the Holy Bible, New International Version®, NIV®. Copyright © 1973, 1978, 1984, 2011 by Biblica, Inc.™ Used by permission of Zondervan. All rights reserved worldwide. *www.zondervan.com*. The "NIV" and "New International Version" are trademarks registered in the United States Patent and Trademark Office by Biblica, Inc.™

Groove Team

Neil M. Alexander: Publisher
Marjorie M. Pon: Editor, Church School Publications
Jack Radcliffe: Managing Editor
Jason Sansbury: Editor
Sheila K. Hewitt: Production Editing Supervisor
Pam Shepherd: Production Editor
Keely Moore: Design Manager
Kellie Green: Designer
Tony Akers: Writer
Kevin Crawford: Devotional Writer

15 16 17 18 19 20 21 22 23 24 — 10 9 8 7 6 5 4 3 2 1

Contents

About This *Groove* Study 5

How to Use *Groove* 7

About The *Groove* Student Journal 9

Week 1: Morals and Ethics 11

Week 2: The Love Commandment 21

Week 3: Valuing Values 31

Week 4: Choices and Consequences 41

About This *Groove* Study

Every day, youth are called to navigate a world full of challenging choices—from the simple choices about everyday life to the much more serious ethical dilemmas that can make being a teenager such a complicated experience. So how do we help them as they seek to make choices that are consistent with their character and their faith?

Groove: Dilemmas is a four-week Bible study designed to help the teens in your ministry understand how to make inspired, smart choices that reflect both who they are and who they are striving to become. What does it mean to be a person with established morals and ethics? How does the commandment to love others affect our lives in a tangible way? How do we live into the values that we claim as followers of Jesus? And what happens when we make choices that have consequences that greatly affect our lives and the lives of those around us?

Dilemmas isn't designed to give simple answers to complicated questions. The study's sessions and the daily devotions of the *Groove: Dilemmas Student Journal* will challenge the youth to be deliberate, thoughtful, and faithful as they work through the choices that they have to make.

Thank you for using *Groove: Dilemmas* and for challenging teens to live faithful, thoughtful lives as they seek to follow Jesus!

How to Use *Groove*

The *Groove* curriculum was designed to help you lead a great gathering of teens, providing enough material for you, as the youth leader, to choose the pieces that work well for your group and that guide the teens into discussion, helping to integrate their faith into their daily lives. The format is designed to teach and engage as well as to prompt teens to wrestle with and ask hard questions. To that end, below are some explanations about the format, layout, and ways to best use the resource.

The Key Format Components

Gather Up

As the teens arrive for each session, first impressions say everything about how you are prepared to welcome them. In addition to creating a warm, teen-friendly environment, most lessons will include an activity to engage teens directly and move their mindset toward the more organized structure of the lesson. Because teens occasionally arrive late, this activity is intentionally designed so that a teen may arrive during or after it without being lost or behind during the remaining session time.

Warm Up

As you and your group transition from the active or welcoming part of Gather Up, you want to prime the pump of your teens' hearts and minds. This usually happens in an activity that helps them to focus on the subject of the lesson. The activity is meant to be short and to engage and set up what comes next.

Look Up

This section is the direct teaching time of the lesson. Included is the teaching outline, which correlates with the student journal activities, as well as some background and additional information to help teach a concise lesson. You will notice that the Look Up section rarely ever finishes a lesson or "puts a bow on it," so to speak. The teaching builds to a place where the teens participate in what comes next: discussion.

Talk Up

Teens will engage and share in this section. If your group is large, you may choose to divide the teens into small groups or teams during this activity and then come back together afterward. If your group is small, you may choose to shift from guiding the lesson yourself to allowing teens to guide and shape it. Included are small-group questions, reflections, and exercises to deepen the learning for and with the teens.

Wrap Up

This section concludes your group meeting. It is intentionally designed to include an activity, a thought, or a prayer that will move teens from a group discussion to personal consideration for their daily lives.

Lace Them Up

This section challenges teens to think about how the truths of this lesson apply in their lives for the next days and weeks to come.

About the
Groove Student Journal

The *Groove* Student Journal has a singular purpose: to provide an easy-to-use tool for your teens and to help them reflect deeply and process what they are learning and how they are growing both during youth gatherings and beyond.

The journal for each week includes fill-in-the-blank activities and questions for the Talk Up and Wrap Up portions of the lesson. In addition, there are discussion prompts for small groups.

While what happens in your youth gatherings is incredibly valuable, most spiritual formation in teenagers takes place outside of your youth gathering. It is in the classroom, with friends, at practice, walking to class, with family, when making decisions, or in the quiet moments alone where deep consideration of faith commitments occurs.

Connecting what is taught and learned at youth group with the rest of life is easier said than done. Every situation mentioned above provides an opportunity to choose to follow Christ. The *Groove* Student Journal includes twenty devotions (five per lesson) to help your teens continue their faith formation beyond youth group and make the most of their opportunities.

Morals and Ethics

Sum Up

Scripture provides guidelines for knowing right and wrong.

Scripture References: Exodus 20:1-17; Psalm 119:9; Matthew 7:12

Key Verse

Therefore, you should treat people in the same way that you want people to treat you. (Matthew 7:12)

Parent E-mail

The psalmist in Psalm 119:9 asks an important question: "How can young people keep their path pure?" As adults, we can easily find ourselves thankful that we didn't grow up with the same pressures that our children face. Granted, we had our own moral dilemmas, but most of our mistakes took place in public. We were being watched by teachers, neighbors, and relatives; and despite our best efforts to keep our mistakes hidden from our parents, they likely found out about those mistakes through those sources.

Our teens live *privately in public*—group texts, secret online searches, and daily communication with people through their phones and social media that their parents will likely never meet or even discover. How can our teens deal with the stream of darkness and negativity that comes to them every day through their online life alone? "How can young people keep their path pure?"

Notes

This week begins a series that addresses how Scripture can inform moral and ethical dilemmas. We hope your teen can join us. Please pray for us as we gather this week.

Leader Note

Psalm 119:9 asks the question: "How can young people keep their path pure?" As adults working with teens, we ask: How can our teens keep themselves pure in a world where pornography downloads create more revenue than all professional sports combined? How can young people keep themselves pure when texts from "friends" include inappropriate pictures or statements? Most decisions—moral and otherwise—that our young people make are influenced by family, peer group, school, society, and organizations to which they belong (one reason our youth ministry is so important). Despite what some people think, most teens, especially younger teens, do wish to please those around them. We all long to be accepted and affirmed by those we respect. Learning to make positive moral and ethical decisions requires a village of caring and loving adults willing to share life with young people. Your affirmation and love literally is leading them to make great decisions. The psalmist answers his own question: "By guarding them according to what you've said [God's Word]."

What influences—positive or negative—do you see operating in the lives of the teens who will attend this study? Are these influences allowing God's Word to shape their moral and ethical decisions?

Finally, think about each teen in your group and pray for him or her as you prepare to lead this week.

Theology and the Topic

Theology simply means the "study of God." We study God through our personal experiences with God, through the experiences of others, and through our study of the Bible. God's love for us, our love for God, and the study of God call us to be the kind of people God originally intended. One of life's great lessons is learning that we are not alone. When we open our eyes, we encounter God's presence in a variety of ways—especially as we experience love, compassion, guidance, and inspiration from those around us. Their love reflects God's love.

A community of faith shares our burdens, supports us, and creates opportunities for us to learn more about God. When we walk through Scripture with our teens, we help them make connections and provide anchor points for their faith. Not every modern moral dilemma can be directly addressed in Scripture, but we can help our teens make connections that allow them to respond faithfully *as Christians* in the midst of these dilemmas.

Leader Reflection

How often can we hear the Ten Commandments without our eyes glazing over from familiarity? Your challenge this week is to pray for God to help you see the commandments with new eyes. Consider the following questions:

- *How do the commandments illuminate how we are to interact with God? with others?*
- *Do you take the moral guidelines of the commandments seriously?*
- *How has grace shaped your resolve to keep the commandments?*

The challenge this week as a leader will be to walk the line of law and grace with your teens. We cannot keep the commandments apart from the grace of God. In that way, the commandments actually show us how dependent we are on grace. Teens will likely wish to focus on the dos and don'ts and seek formulaic answers to difficult issues. Push them to think deeper and to seek grace as a guide to keep the commandments and not make God's grace an excuse to ignore them.

Supplies Needed

- Handouts for each participant (See page 20.)
- Pen and sheet of paper for each teen
- Sheet of paper with a large question mark on it
- A bag of candy

Gather Up

High Energy Option: Find Ten

This is a super-fast scavenger hunt that can be noisy. So check on the presence of other people or groups and set boundaries accordingly.

Each team's goal is to be first to "find ten" of the same items in the church and return them to your meeting space. Divide participants into groups of three or four. The first team back with ten items that are the same wins. Give candy to the winner.

Variations

- Creativity is encouraged. Teams may bring back different items if they can make logical connections between each item.
- Play a round just in the meeting area.
- Play with just the items in their wallets or purses.

Debrief Questions

- *What was difficult about this game?*
- *Would it have been easier if there had been fewer than ten items? Why or why not?*

Low Energy Option: Can You Follow Instructions?

Before group time, create handouts for your group of the "Instructions," on page 20. Give each teen a pen, a sheet of paper, and the instruction sheet. Explain that it's a race, and the winner receives candy. Set a timer for three minutes and say, "Go!"

If the teens read all of the directions, they will write *only* their names on their Instructions sheet. If they skip the instructions, it will become painfully obvious that they did not follow instructions.

Copy this exactly as it appears for your handouts:

Debrief Questions

- *What was difficult about this game?*
- *What kept you from reading all the way through the guidelines?*
- *Were you more concerned with winning or following the directions?*

Give candy to those who wrote only their name.

Warm Up

A Rule of Life

Say: "We all have rules or guidelines that we follow in our daily lives. Some of those rules are shaped by laws, some by our parents, and some by our own quirkiness. Most of the time, the guidelines we commit to are set by us because we have had a negative or positive experience related to them. Let's list some of the rules we commit to that make life better not only for us but also for others."

Examples:

- I throw away litter, and I recycle.
- I return the shopping cart to the store when I'm finished with it.
- I always fill the gas tank when it's half full.
- I always say please and thank you.
- I don't ask anyone to do anything I wouldn't do.

Ask:

- *When you have a moral dilemma or an ethical decision, where in Scripture do you seek guidance?*

Say: "Most Christians turn to the Ten Commandments when they think about moral decision-making. Let's explore the challenges of the Ten Commandments."

Look Up

The Big Ten: Version 2.0

As a group, read Exodus 20:1-17, the Ten Commandments. As you read, address terms teens may not understand in each commandment. Say something for each, such as, "What is *sabbath*?"

Leader Audible

Don't assume that your teens know what *adultery* or *covet* mean. When addressing the concept of adultery, simply say that a married man or woman is acting or living as if someone else is his or her spouse. Be aware that many of your teens may be affected by divorce. Because we are discussing "commandments," younger teens, especially, may equate divorce with an unforgivable act. Here you'll have the opportunity to talk about how the The Commandments make us aware of our dependence on God and God's grace. Assure teens that God's forgiveness is available to all.

Divide the group into five teams of two or more people. Assign each team two of the Ten Commandments. Allow ten minutes to rewrite them in terms that someone their age would understand, without losing the original meaning.

When the assignment is completed, call on each team to share its results. Then ask:

- *Why did God give these instructions?*
- *How does obeying the Ten Commandments give us freedom?*
- *Are there certain commandments that are taken more seriously than the others?*
- *Which commandment is easiest to ignore? Why?*
- *When they are broken, do some commandments have more serious consequences than others?*
- *Were the commandments written for Jews or Christians? Does it matter?*
- *What, do you think, would happen if everyone were to obey the Ten Commandments?*

Talk Up

Scratch and Sniff: What Lies Beneath?

Each commandment is ripe with spiritual and practical guidance. If we aren't careful, we can miss the depth of each commandment by taking it at face value. Each commandment speaks specifically to relationships. The first four commandments speak to one's relationship with God. The final six commandments speak to one's relationship with others. Each commandment is built upon the foundation of relationships and how to function in community. How do we value others?

Say: "Is it possible to follow the letter of the law and not the spirit of the law? For instance, Jesus says in Matthew 5:28 that 'every man who looks at a woman lustfully has already committed adultery in his heart.' How can we obey the rule of the law and miss the spirit of the law?

"For example: Exodus 20:12 says, 'Honor your father and your mother.' Saturday is cleaning day, and your family has multiple chores to do. Your parents ask you to clean your room. You clean your room slowly all day so that you don't have to help with other chores. Technically, your room has been cleaned, but did you honor your father and mother?"

Ask the teens to return to their teams to create for both of their commandments a scenario that highlights the rule of the law and the spirit of the law. Teams will share their scenarios with the group.

Ask:

- *How does honoring the spirit of the law bring value to our relationship to God and others?*

Wrap Up

Go for the Gold

Read aloud Matthew 7:12.

Ask:

- *This verse is considered the "Golden Rule." Have you heard of it? Why is this rule golden?*

- *If we were to keep the Golden Rule, would we not also keep the commandments? Why, or why not?*
- *Are the Ten Commandments and the Golden Rule significant in today's society? If so, how? If not, why?*

Point out that most decisions in life need more than a flip of the coin for positive outcomes.

Challenge participants to pay attention to any dilemmas they encounter during the week and to practice using the Ten Commandments and the Golden Rule as they deal with the problems.

Prayer

A Firm Foundation

Ask youth to stand in a circle. Draw a large question mark on a sheet of paper and put it on the floor (or table or altar) in the center of the group.

Say: "Life is full of questions. We may want to do what is right, good, and just, but we may not always be certain of what that is and how to decide."

Now lay a Bible on top of the question mark.

Say: "We are not without help when we face moral or ethical dilemmas. In the coming week, remember that God's Word provides a firm foundation." Circle up and say a closing prayer.

Give the teens candy as they leave, reminding them that God's grace is available when we break a commandment and that "do-overs" are available through God's amazing grace.

Instructions

Read all of the instructions before doing anything. You are allowed three minutes to complete this task, but the person to finish first is the winner.

1. Write your name at the top of the sheet of paper.
2. Number the sheet of paper from 1 to 5.
3. Draw five small circles beside #1.
4. Be creative and make the five small circles into flowers.
5. Write the word *burrito* beside #2.
6. On the back of the paper, multiply 10 by 17.
7. Put an X in the lower right-hand corner of the front of the paper.
8. Draw a circle around the X you just made.
9. Underline your whole name.
10. Say your name out loud.
11. Draw a circle around #3.
12. Quickly count to 50 out loud.
13. Draw a square around #1 and #5.
14. Put your paper on the floor and stand on it.
15. Write your first name beside #4.
16. Write today's date beside #5.
17. Fold your paper in half four times and put in one of your armpits.
18. Stand up, strike a pose, and declare: "I am the winner!"
19. Write your name on this instruction paper. Ignore the other instructions.

The Love Commandment

Sum Up

In the love commandment, Jesus provided an anchor point for us in our moral decision-making.

Scripture References: Matthew 22:36-40; Luke 6:27-36; 1 John 4:7-8

Key Verse

Dear friends, let's love each other, because love is from God.
(1 John 4:7a)

Parent E-mail

How do teens deal with gray areas in their moral decision-making? In the wisdom of God and through Jesus, we were given what has been called the "Love Commandment" as the foundation for the Christian life and moral decision-making: "You must love the Lord your God with all your heart, with all your being, and with all your mind. This is the first and greatest commandment. And the second is like it: You must love your neighbor as you love yourself. All the Law and the Prophets depend on these two commands" (Matthew 22:37-40).

Our teens are constantly thinking about and seeking love and affirmation. Many question how God could love them, how peers could love them, and may even wonder whether parents love them.

This week we will challenge our teens to think of *love* as both a noun and a verb and to use it as a foundation for all they are, for all they do, and for all they decide. Please pray for us as we gather this week.

Leader Note

How do teens handle gray areas in their moral decision-making? Some want to swim in the shallow water of an unreflected faith. "God said _____" becomes an easy out that shortcuts moral and spiritual development. Others have cut the moorings of Scripture as a guide and are looking everywhere but faith to form and inform their decision-making. As leaders, we are in a position to speak to both extremes. How can we challenge those who do not reflect deeply and reel in those who have jettisoned scriptural truth for the current of culture?

In the wisdom of God and through Jesus, we were given the "Love Commandment." Read Matthew 22:36-40. Helping teens embrace the truth that everyone deserves love can be a huge challenge. We must help teens recognize that loving acts done in sincerity literally can become reflections of God's love to others.

How do we address moral decision-making with our teens? A loving response to a struggling teen can open the door to the love of God and a relationship with Jesus. Teens want to be loved and to know they are lovable. Help them look beyond themselves and at others, and to embrace Jesus' teachings as the ultimate model of love.

Theology and the Topic

The Scriptures reveal the intention of God and the will of God. God's love fills us; and in turn, we are called to reflect that love—a love that is all-consuming, encompassing, and leads us in a couple of different directions:

To God—we are commanded to love God with all we are, body and soul. We are told that this is the greatest commandment. From this commandment the second commandment flows.

To Others—God's love leads us to love others as we love ourselves. We are challenged to "see" others with the same value as ourselves. The two commands express the essence of the Torah, the first five books of the Hebrew Bible (Old Testament).

We must think of *love* as both a noun and a verb, to use it as a foundation for all that we are and all that we do. God calls us to think and act out of love. God calls us to be love. Love is not a single act but ongoing obedience, compassion, effort, and responsibility.

Leader Reflection

Matthew 22:37: "You must love the Lord your God with all your heart, with all your being, and with all your mind." Is love the foundation for why you serve in this teen ministry? the cornerstone upon which you build? your North Star that guides your life and ministry? How does this command to love shape your life as you seek to shape the lives of others?

Matthew 22:39: "You must love your neighbor as yourself." Who are our neighbors? How do we *become* neighbors? Are all we encounter our neighbors? We become neighbors when we perform acts of concern and compassion. Are we good neighbors?

Luke 6:27-28: "But I say to you who are willing to hear: Love your enemies. Do good to those who hate you. Bless those who curse you. Pray for those who mistreat you." Do we love only those who are lovable? Loving those we consider as enemies is a difficult teaching of Jesus. Does Jesus ask us out on a limb only to cut it off? No way! There are rewards to loving our enemies. We are freed from the bondage of hate when we can care for those who don't deserve it. How are you showing love to those who do not deserve it?

1 John 4:7: "Dear friends, let's love each other, because love is from God, and everyone who loves is born from God and knows God." Love comes from God. We don't manufacture it. We can only live in obedience to God's command to love—a love that God provides. By demonstrating the love of God, we grow in our ability to witness to the love *of* God. How have you experienced the love of God through the church? through other believers? How are you relying on God to provide the love that others need to experience through you?

Supplies Needed

- A long length of rope
- Four clothespins for each participant
- A black permanent marker for each participant
- Several old magazines

Gather Up

High Energy Option: Give It Away

As teens enter the room, give each of them four clothespins and tell them to clip them on their sleeves. When everyone has entered, explain the object of the game: to get the clothespins off of you and onto others. They may put clothespins only on loose clothing. Set a one-minute time limit. On "go" the teens will try to pin others while dodging being pinned. At the conclusion of the game, note teens with the least pins and the most pins.

Game Option

Play music as a "timer." Turn off the song when you are ready to count the pins.

Game Debrief

- *What was difficult about this game?*
- *What frustrated you the most?*
- *Was it difficult to give away something that keeps coming back to you?*

Low Energy Option: Tethered Together

Bring out a long length of rope and explain that teens will use it to make shapes. Ask everyone to stand and grab a portion of the rope. Then say, "Make the shape of a triangle." The teens will then make a triangle shape with the rope. When finished, congratulate them on their success. Now ask them to close their eyes and make the same triangle shape. Debrief the experience and discuss why it was difficult and how to improve. Do it a third time instructing teens to close their eyes; also include a "no talking" rule.

Game Debrief

- *What was difficult about this game?*
- *Did being connected with others help or hinder the success of your team? How?*
- *What would have made it easier for teams to communicate their positions within the shape?*
- *Did you struggle to follow the lead of others? Why?*

The Love Commandment

Warm Up

Branded Love

Divide the group into teams of three or four and hand out magazines. Allow teams 3–5 minutes to rip out ads that communicate love. Call on teams to tell how their ads promote love. If they defend their ads well, they get a point. (Other groups may point out weak arguments.) The team with the most defended ads wins. You may allow one team to judge if points will be awarded. Allow teams to argue their points from a "worldly" point of view if you wish.

Ask:

- *How do the pictures represent love in correct ways? in incorrect and confusing ways?*
- *Did you assume that this activity was about romantic love? Why, or why not?*
- *Do any of the ads represent to you God's command to "Love one another"?*

A Rule of Love

Say: "Is love a commitment to what is best for others or a feeling we have toward those we care about? The word *love* can represent many different things—love of food, romantic love, selfish love, selfless love—the list is endless. John Wesley (founder of Methodism) developed three "General Rules" to express love in our relationship with God and others. These rules were grounded in and shaped by love:

- Do no harm.
- Do good.
- Stay in love with God.

As a group, spend some time establishing a "rule of love" that would help your teens understand God's unconditional love. Try to come up with three rules that would best help define the love of God expressed through the teens.

Then say: "Today we are going to look at one of God's most challenging commands—the command to love God with all we are and to love others as well. The Scriptures we are about to read make the point that Christian morality and decision-making is not just about the Ten Commandments or any other set of rules. Instead, Christian morality and decision-making is based on love. Let's examine what Scripture says about love."

Look Up

Two-Scene Skits

Divide the group into four teams. Assign each team one of these Scriptures: Matthew 22:37; Matthew 22:39; Luke 6:27-28; 1 John 4:7. Teams will tie their Scripture into a two-scene skit about a moral dilemma a teen might face. When teams have written and practiced their scenes, call on them to present the skits and tell how their Scripture addresses the dilemma.

Leader Audible

Teens will discuss the Scripture and dilemmas teens may face. After each skit, ask questions that will help teens process the information. Affirm all answers that reveal serious thought and consideration.

Skit Example: Matthew 22:37

Scene 1: Jack hasn't studied for his history test. It's really late, and he's discouraged. He closes his books in frustration and goes to sleep.

Scene 2: The next morning, Jack asks his friend Sam to leave his test paper where he can copy it. Sam refuses.

Scripture Tie-in: "You must love the Lord your God with all your heart, with all your being, and *with all your mind*" (emphasis added).

Ask:

- *Were the dilemmas addressed in the skits something you would encounter? How so?*
- *What were the similarities of the Scriptures that each skit highlighted?*
- *How does a commitment to love shape the way we make moral decisions?*
- *Do you see wisdom in God's command to love? Why, or why not?*

Talk Up

Bad-Awful-The Worst

Label three areas in your meeting space: "Bad," "Awful," and "The Worst." Explain that you'll read a series of three somewhat-related statements. As you read aloud each statement, allow teens to decide whether it is bad, awful, or the worst and move to the area of the room that represents their choice. Take time to discuss their individual choices. Allow for healthy debate. This activity helps identify how our teens express values and how decisions are influenced by our love and concern for others.

1. Talking bad behind someone's back
2. Talking bad about someone to his or her face
3. Ignoring someone

1. Borrowing someone else's homework
2. Copying from someone during a test
3. Not studying for a test
1. Breaking your curfew
2. Telling your parents that curfews are stupid
3. Sneaking in the window after curfew
1. Tweeting something that is not true
2. Having a relationship with someone on social media without your parents knowing
3. Tweeting something true but shouldn't be said
1. Yelling at a friend to return borrowed money
2. Sneaking and going through your friend's purse or wallet to get your money back
3. Telling others that the friend who borrowed the money cannot be trusted
1. Texting in class
2. Texting while driving during rush hour
3. Texting when you are supposed to be asleep

Debrief Questions

- *How does our concern for others shape our moral decision-making in the scenarios we discussed?*
- *How does a lack of concern shape our moral decision-making?*

Wrap Up

Give It Away (Revisited)

Redistribute four clothespins and a black permanent marker to each participant.

Say: "Loving God with all our hearts is our starting place, cornerstone, foundation, and North Star that leads us to discover who we are. The incredible news of God's love, often taken for granted by Christians, is one that is desperately needed in our world. The natural expression of God's love toward us is to 'love our neighbors as ourselves.' How can we show concern for those we consider neighbors? The smallest of acts can open a door to God's love. On the clothespins we have given you, write four affirmations you can share with others. Here are some examples:

- Great smile!
- God loves you!
- You are cool!
- You are someone's hero!

"During the day tomorrow share these affirmations with others by secretly clipping them to their loose clothing. If you get caught, simply share that you were challenged at youth group to affirm others. You might use this time to invite them to your youth group or begin a conversation about faith."

Prayer
Tethered

Ask teens to gather in the center of the meeting space and reintroduce the rope from the earlier activity. Ask each person to hold the rope and then make the shape of a cross (eyes open this time).

Say: "We are bound together, or tethered, by God's love for us and our love and concern for one another. When one of us experiences a joy, it is multiplied by us. When one of us experiences pain and shares that pain, it is lessened among us as we bear burdens for others."

Take time to express joys and prayer concerns. When everyone has had a chance to participate in the conversation, close in prayer.

Valuing Values

Sum Up

The Scriptures and Jesus' life shape who we are and what we value as Christians.

Scripture References: Micah 6:8; Matthew 25:34-40; Galatians 5:22-23; Philippians 4:8-9

Key Verse

Practice these things: whatever you learned, received, heard, or saw in us. The God of peace will be with you. (Philippians 4:9)

Parent E-mail

Never before have we had more information about what it means to be a Christian and more challenges in living faithfully. Parents need to be in the affirmation business. As you hold on to the bicycle seat, you need to steady and to provide the confidence of your presence as your teen takes tentative cranks on the pedals of his or her faith.

What are some noticeable improvements you have observed as your teen lives out his or her Christian values? Affirm those improvements. Give voice to the growth that you see in his or her faith. As your teen fights the current of culture, give him or her confidence that he or she does not swim alone, because you are fighting the current right along with your teen. Please pray for us as we gather this week.

Leader Note

We have a big challenge: to help our teens embrace the particulars of the faith and live it out in a culture that, for the most part, doesn't value the commitments of Christians or even recognize why those commitments are vital. Our culture values retribution over "turning the other cheek." We see "shaming" behavior online. Teens live with "subtweets" that anonymously call out unnamed "others" online, leaving those who read them to wonder whether they are being targeted. We live in an image-obsessed culture that worries about "thigh gaps," social media "likes," and waist-to-hip ratios. We live in a culture that perpetuates immediate gratification and immediate access to information.

What are some noticeable improvements you've observed as your teens live out Christian values? Has your group grown closer? Do they listen more intently as others share? Do your group members get along? How do your teens feel about themselves? Give voice and affirmation to the growth you see in their faith.

Theology and the Topic

Christian values help us identify right and wrong. Left to our own devices, we'll almost always return to the default setting of *self*. To do so harms others; damages personal integrity; and doesn't reflect the love of Christ for our neighbors, enemies, or the community of faith.

Some dilemmas pit good against good or even "could be" right against "could be" right or wrong. Given the complexity of life, not only choices but also values may be in conflict or be unclear. Our faith is based on loving God and others. God's freely given love compels us to be more loving. On occasion, we can do injustice to God's gift of love by reducing life's challenges and dilemmas to cheap questions and cheap answers. Examples: putting self first, failing to seek God, telling others to do what we do not practice ourselves, limiting the whole of a person to a "sound bite," when we see things only our way.

In contrast, when we turn to the things we value—God's love, God's Word, Christian tradition, and our ability to do theology by faithfully committing to study and reason—we experience a life-sustaining faith. A faith rooted in God's love for us and others positions us to tackle dilemmas and difficult choices.

Leader Reflection

You are loved by God and are given opportunities to serve, which God prepared for you to do (Ephesians 2:10). How has your leadership in ministry to teens challenged you and your faith? Have you embraced your position as one prepared just for you? How do you experience God's love being reflected through you to the teens? How do you experience God's love reflected back to you from them?

"He has told you, human one, what is good and /what the LORD requires from you: / to do justice, embrace faithful love, and walk humbly with your God" (Micah 6:8). The Bible teaches us to be humble, compassionate, kind, patient, and gentle. Our thoughts and actions are right when we love God and our neighbors. When we walk side-by-side with our teens, God encourages us to continue with "faithful love." We will need this mindset as we watch our teens stumble along their journey. Are they really that different from us? No! If you give yourself grace in your journey of faith (and you should), why can't you continue to walk with your teens in grace? In what ways are you giving grace to your teens while encouraging them onward?

Our teens will "know we are Christians by our love." No good deed is unnoticed by them. When we "let the word of Christ . . . live in [us] richly" (Colossians 3:16), we will find God's Word transforming our minds and hearts and giving us a deeper commitment to walk faithfully in front of our teens. Your witness to them means more than you'll know.

Supplies Needed

- Newspaper, tape, and trash can
- Sheet of posterboard, large sheet of paper, or a markerboard for every four to five teens and appropriate markers
- Sheets of paper cut in half or large index cards
- Pens or pencils

Gather Up

High Energy Option: Bludger Ball

Ahead of time, create several paper "bludger" batons from rolled-up newspaper wrapped in tape. Make the batons at least two feet long and sturdy.

Introduce the game (*bludger* is a Harry Potter Quiddich term). Put a trash can in the middle of your playing area. Divide the group into three teams. Choose one team to lie down around the trash can like the spokes of a wheel, with heads closest to the trash can, and give each person a bludger. Each of the other teams takes two minutes to try to toss wads of newspaper into the can while

bludger wavers bat away the flying wads. Rotate so
that each team gets a turn with the bludgers. After
each round, count the wads of paper in the can.
The team with the fewest wads in the can while they
were defending it is declared the winner.

Debrief Questions

- *What was difficult about this game?*
- *Was it more fun to toss or defend? Why?*

Low Energy Option: Origins

Sit with teens in a circle. Ask for a volunteer to be
"It," then "It" leaves the room. Post someone by
the door so that "It" cannot see in or hear. Select
an "Origin" to guide the rest of the group in a series
of motions. Call "It" back into the room and tell
him or her to identify the Origin of the motions. The
Origin slyly starts some motion, such as waving
a hand, nodding a head, making a face, wiggling
fingers, clapping hands, or crossing legs. Everyone
should immediately imitate Origin, without staring
at him or her. Origin changes motions frequently.
"It" has three guesses to discover who Origin is.
When Origin is guessed correctly, another volunteer
becomes "It." Play several rounds.

Debrief Questions

- *What was difficult about this game?*
- *As a participant, was it difficult to follow the
  leader without revealing who it was?*

Warm Up

Discuss these questions:

- *In terms of character, what is a value?*
- *What values do you look for in friends?*

Handwritten notes:
What values do you have?
Would you ever compromise them?
Your values will be tested

- *What values would you want in a mechanic? Are they the same as the qualities for a friend? Why?*
- *What values should be evident in Christians?*

Posterize Your Values

Divide the group into four teams. Give each team a posterboard and some markers to "create" a Christian. Teams will draw a body and write values next to each part of the body. For instance: Head—fill our minds with good things; hands—serve others; knees—humble myself to pray; heart—show compassion.

Leader Audible

Ask teams to share their posters. Highlight any of the values below that were not mentioned:

- Sacred worth of all human beings • Truth
- Community • Compassion and caring for others
- Justice/treating others fairly • Respect
- Service to others • Self-denial and sacrifice
- Freedom • Responsibility • Commitment
- Humility • Taking care of what you have
- Sharing what you have• Forgiveness • Faith
- Treating one's body as the temple of God
- Personal integrity • Human dignity • Hope

Look Up

Values—Before and After

Hand out a large index card or a half sheet of paper and a pen or pencil to each teen. Ask teens to number one side of the card from 1 to 10. Ask them to rank the following scenarios from 1 (no big deal) to 5 (Christians don't do this).

- Filling pockets with "free" mints at a restaurant
- Keeping secret that a friend has an eating disorder
- Borrowing prescription medication to help you focus on a test
- Keeping fast-food cups to help yourself to refills
- Hiding formulas in a calculator to cheat on a test
- Checking social media while driving
- Consistently skipping worship
- Asking an adult to buy you a lottery ticket
- Visiting "adult" websites
- Hiding the fact that you are a Christian

Say: "As we read the following Scriptures, think about your rankings."

Ask teens to read aloud the following Scriptures without comment: Micah 6:8; Matthew 25:34-40; Galatians 5:22-23; Philippians 4:8-9. Ask everyone to turn over his or her card and number it 1 to 10.

Reread the list of scenarios and ask teens to rank them based on what they heard in the Scriptures.

Ask:

- *Did your rankings change? Why, or why not?*

Say: "The Scriptures provide a rich tapestry of help when it comes to identifying and including values in our lives. If our brief time spent with the Scripture has changed our decisions regarding values, consider how much more they are likely to change if we seek scriptural guidance in every dilemma we face.

Ask:

- *Are you seeking out Scripture to shape your values? Why, or why not?*

Talk Up

God, Others, Self

Encourage the teens to draw the symbol for the Trinity (three intersecting circles) and to designate the circles as "God values," "my values," and "peer values." The center section is to highlight common values for God, others, and self. Allow five minutes to do this.

Leader Audible

Provide the list of God's values used earlier if teens are struggling. At the end of five minutes, encourage participants to pair up and give them another five minutes to discuss commonalities and differences in values.

Ask:

- *Why is it important to discuss the differences in values between Christian teens and their peers?*

Say: "Sometimes we aren't aware of what our peers value until we put it on paper. This isn't an exercise to create an 'us versus them' mentality, but it's an opportunity to highlight common values. Awareness of these common values can provide a beginning point for conversations, to make friends, and maybe even to talk about faith."

Wrap Up

Bludgers and Origins (Revisited)

Say: "We kicked off the lesson with a few games. Bludger Ball was a challenging game to protect your area (trash can) from what others were throwing at it. In a similar way, the world is throwing their values at us. We can let some through—the importance of friends, family, and so on, but there are other world values that we need to develop a quick response to reject. How do we do that?

"Consider the Origins game. While we were playing Origins, we were literally taking our cues from elsewhere. As Christians, we need to continue to seek God's cues through Scripture study, worship, and prayer—and commit to God's values to guide and shape our personal values.

"It is important that as we discuss values we don't degenerate so much into what we believe but instead focus on why we believe what we do. Keeping God and Scripture in the forefront of that discussion provides a solid foundation for us as we move forward identifying and committing to values."

Prayer

Gather the "Christian" posters created earlier and place them in the middle of the floor where they can be seen. Circle the group around the posters and encourage them to pick out a value they see illustrated on the posters that they would like to see in their life. Begin a "go around" prayer. As prayer moves around the circle, encourage the teens to complete this sentence, "God, help me to value _____." When the prayer returns to you, close in prayer, affirming all that was offered to God.

Choices and Consequences

Sum Up

As Christians we make choices that honor God and others.

Scripture References: Genesis 3:1-24; James 1:5

Key Verse

> The LORD God commanded the human, "Eat your fill from all of the garden's trees; but don't eat from the tree of the knowledge of good and evil." (Genesis 2:16)

Parent E-mail

We like to talk about blame. Everyone wants to place blame, and no one wants to accept blame. Even when we own up to making poor decisions, that doesn't mean we are open to consequences. Our default setting is to deflect blame or, better yet, to blame someone else. We want to be considered blameless and pretend that the problem does not exist. Sounds a lot like what happened in the garden of Eden. Sounds a lot like teens, doesn't it?

Our session this week explores choices and consequences. We will discuss some tools to help our teens make wise, God-honoring decisions. Please pray for us as we gather this week!

Leader Note

No one can justify actions better than teens. When they are blamed, they become miniature attorneys, arguing their defense to whomever will listen. Amazingly, teens actually believe their own press.

Their toughest choices are shaped by their peers. Faced with such pressure, teens need the skills to weigh choices and consequences in light of their faith. Recent brain research has revealed that our brains are forming until the age of 25. The last area to form is the frontal cortex, which controls the ability to choose and to discern cause and effect. That doesn't mean that teens cannot choose; it simply means that they need coaching along the way.

This session explores choices and consequences. You can help teens by pointing out that even positive choices can have unpleasant consequences. Embrace your role as "coach" this week as you lead your teens.

Theology and the Topic

What we see in our Scripture today is an opportunity to live in freedom. Given the chance, our newly created ancestors from long ago chose disobedience. To be fair, they were pretty new at this whole "life" thing. But would you and I have made a better choice, given the same opportunity? We may have struggled to do the right thing as well.

When are we truly free? We are most free when we choose obedience to God's love. Disobedience shackles us; indifference weighs us down. But love and responsibility free us. Chaos and confusion reign when we are disobedient, and it is difficult (though not impossible because of grace) to recover.

The early church understood that to be disobedient to God was to sin. *Sin* was an archery term that meant one "missed the mark." When an archer missed the bull's-eye, onlookers would yell, "sin up," or "sin down," to help the archer find his or her mark. We seek the bull's-eye of obedience. We seek to love God with all that we are and to love our neighbors as ourselves. When we walk within these boundaries, we experience freedom. Thankfully, when we miss the mark we can repent and make new choices because of God's forgiveness and grace. In the love of God and in God's precepts we find our freedom.

Leader Reflection

Making any choice is not easy. Our culture has elevated choices to the point of distraction. Even though we are highly trained as consumers, we are not necessarily ready to choose well in matters of the heart. Sometimes the consequences—good or bad—are unclear. Sometimes we simply lack the courage to choose rightly. Knowing the difference between good and evil helps us avoid wrong paths. Our Scripture passage reminds us to be aware of temptation and consequences.

Read Genesis 2:16–3:24. Ask yourself the following:

- *How are the limitations that God places on us assets and not liabilities?*
- *Can you recall any wise choices you have made that observed limits? What about any foolish choices you made by ignoring boundaries?*
- *When you make poor choices, how do you "hide" from God?*
- *How has God cared for you after bad choices?*
- *How were you restored?*

Supplies Needed

- Deck of playing cards.
- Bag of candy
- Letter tiles from a game such as Scrabble®
- Index card or scrap paper and a pen for each teen
- Markerboard and appropriate markers

Gather Up

High Energy Option: Group Poker

Hand teens playing cards as they arrive. Be sure to hand out all of the cards. As you call out various combinations of Poker hands, teens are to quickly move to create that hand with other players. Do a primer before the game, of course, since some teens may not know Poker hands. Ask everyone to move to the center of the playing area and then yell out: Two pair, Flush, Four of a kind, Three of a kind, Straight, Full House, and so on. The individuals who create the hand first win that round and a piece of candy. Play several rounds.

Low Energy Option: First Word

Divide your group into teams of four or five. Give each group a handful of letter tiles. Make sure they have plenty of vowels.

Say: "The first team to form a word that might appear on a Mexican restaurant menu wins 1,000 points."

The first team finished shouts, "Done!" If the word fits the category, award points to that team. Continue with random items from random stores or restaurants. The team with the most points at the end wins.

Warm Up

Go Around Question

- *When you have a tough decision or are in a dilemma that requires a choice, what is your process for making God-honoring decisions?*

And Then What?

Divide the group into teams of four or five. Ask each team to think of a real dilemma teens face that requires a decision. The dilemmas could be complicated (A friend asks you to lie about where she or he was Friday night) or less so (A friend asks which college she or he should attend). When they have developed their dilemmas, regather the group.

Teams take turns describing its dilemma, some possible actions, and its choice of action. Then the whole group is asked, "And then what?"

Label the following columns on a markerboard:

Dilemma
Options
Action
Consequences
Potential Outcome

The exercise is to help teens realize that there are consequences to every choice (even good choices). Example:

Dilemma: A friend asks you to lie about where he or she was Friday night.
Options: (1) Tell the truth. (2) Lie. (3) Ask someone for advice.
Action: You tell the truth.

Consequences: (1) You are no longer friends. (2) Your friend apologizes for putting you in that position. (3) You refuse to answer your phone or texts until you think the problem is over.
Potential Outcome: You are no longer friends.

When the consequences plays out, go back to the original options and trace the consequences, choosing a different action. Repeat with each group.

Look Up

Eyewitnesses

Hand out index cards and pens to each teen. Tell the teens to note on the card when they see a choice being presented within the Scripture that you will read. They are to make notes as if they are eyewitnesses who will be interviewed after the fact.

Read aloud Genesis 3:1-24. Then give the teens an opportunity to share the decision points they noted in the Scripture reading.

Ask:

• *How many opportunities did Adam and Eve have to choose wisely?*

Say: "Our freedom to choose is one characteristic that affirms we are created in God's image. But with that free will comes responsibility."

• *Are we doing well with our freedom to choose?*

Say: "God has given each of us the power of choice, the ability to choose among alternatives, between good and evil. But this power means we are accountable for the consequences of our choices."

Ask:

Notes

- *What examples of God's grace are in the story?*

And Then What? (Revisited)

Use the columns from earlier to map Adam and Eve's options. Follow their path to different outcomes.

Ask:

- *How would that story have changed if Adam and Eve had made God-honoring instead of self-honoring decisions? How would the consequences for all of us have changed?*
- *Are our decisions just as important as Adam and Eve's? If so, how would we know?*
- *Did Adam and Eve understand the consequences of their disobedience? Why do you say that?*
- *How can our disobedience be visited upon those who have nothing to do with our decisions?*

Talk Up

Ask:

- *How should being a Christian shape how we make choices?*
- *Are the things we are instructed against in Scripture frustrating to you? Why, or why not?*
- *What wise choices have you made that observed boundaries? What foolish choices have you made by ignoring boundaries?*
- *When you make poor choices, do you (like Adam and Eve) "hide" from God?*
- *How has God cared for you in the aftermath of bad choices?*
- *How do you find restoration when you have made poor choices?*

Wrap Up

Text Choices

Divide the group into two teams and give each team half of the letter tiles. Instruct the teams to create acrostics on the floor to highlight things that help them make good and God-honoring choices.

Then have the teams visit each other's acrostics and discuss how they are helpful when making choices. Encourage the teens to take a photo of their acrostics and use them as a background on their phones to remind them that making good, God-honoring choices are literally in the palm of their hand.

Prayer

Hand each teen a playing card. Remind the class of the Group Poker game.

Say: "We are giving you playing cards to remind you that you are a part of God's 'hand' in the world. Your role in God's kingdom is important, and your choices are important not only to you but to us all. Place this card somewhere you can see it often to remind yourself of that fact.

"God delights when we seek God's wisdom in our decisions. Listen to the promise in this verse."

Read James 1:5: "Anyone who needs wisdom should ask God, whose very nature is to give to everyone without a second thought, without keeping score. Wisdom will certainly be given to those who ask."

Circle up and pray: "God, thank you for the freedom to choose and the grace to seek you in our choices. Help us this week as we encounter choices to seek to honor you in them. Amen."

CPSIA information can be obtained at www.ICGtesting.com
Printed in the USA
LVOW07s0717011115

460488LV00003BA/4/P